Danielle

Love y
Always.

Your Sister
Midge

MW00721293

CHICKEN SOUP FOR THE SOUL®
CELEBRATES SISTERS

CHICKEN SOUP FOR THE SOUL® CELEBRATES SISTERS

A Collection in Words and Photographs by
Jack Canfield and Mark Victor Hansen
and
Maria Bushkin Stave

Health Communications, Inc.
Deerfield Beach, Florida

www.hcibooks.com
www.chickensoup.com

Subject matter, locality and/or people in the photographs may not be the actual locality or people in the stories. Names of certain individuals have been changed to protect their identity.

Library of Congress Cataloging-in-Publication Data

Chicken soup for the soul celebrates sisters : a collection in words and photographs /
  [compiled] by Jack Canfield & Mark Victor Hansen and Maria Bushkin Stave.
    p. cm.
  ISBN 0-7573-0151-7 (tp)
  1. Sisters. 2. Sisters—Family relationships.   I. Canfield, Jack. II. Hansen, Mark Victor.
III. Stave, Maria Bushkin.

BF723.S43C43 2004
306.875'4—dc22

2003056924

Publisher: Health Communications, Inc.
            3201 S.W. 15th Street
            Deerfield Beach, FL 33442-8190

Cover design by Larissa Hise Henoch
Inside formatting by Dawn Von Strolley Grove

CONTENTS

We'll each pick a number, starting from oldest to youngest, then we'll each take a pick, in the order of our numbers. You understand?" Louise was fully in charge. We were taking our pick of Mama's quilts.

None of us wanted to fight. Five sisters and one brother were trying valiantly to honor and respect our parents. Louise is the oldest and had the most daily contact with our mother before her quick death from cancer, long quietly taking over her body, but not loud enough to be noticed until too late. Here we sat, on a cold October day, six middle-aged children in the living room of our youth, with eyes red with grief and nervous sweaty hands.

These last six quilts our mother made were something we

needed to be fair about and they were all laid out for our choosing. Although not works of art for the most part, they were our heritage. There was a queen-size Dresden plate and two twin-size patchworks, both in good shape. A double-size, double-knit polyester little girl quilt that we remembered from the era of leisure suits and a queen-size log cabin that told its age by the colors: orange and avocado. Then there was the quilt on my mother's bed, a double-size star pattern of Wedgwood blue chintz and cotton. It was gorgeous. And it smelled like Mama.

We reached into the shoebox one at a time for our numbers, and being the baby, I picked last. Fitting, as I got number six, the last to choose from the bed-cover legacy. Libby was the first, and no one was surprised to watch her gather up the Wedgwood blue chintz and fold it into her bag. When my turn came, the double-knit polyester quilt was left, so I took it, remembering Mother handstitching the pitiful thing. So much work for so little beauty! *We'll keep it in the car,* I thought to myself, *for a picnic blanket.*

As the holidays approached, our grief stayed with us, mostly hidden, but popping up unannounced as tears over a remembered song or a phone call impossible to make. We all moved our bodies toward Christmas, even as our minds stayed with Mother in her hospital bed before she died, or in her flower garden—or on her sun porch. Christmas would be hard.

Packages began to arrive, though, and I had to notice that the rest of the world didn't stop in the shadow of my sadness. On Christmas Eve, my children have the privilege of opening one package before bed, but on this night they encouraged me to join in. A large box from Ohio had piqued their interest. What could Aunt Libby have sent?

Laughing, I tore open the box, expecting a joke: an inflatable chair or bubble bath buried in yards of newspaper. As I peeked past the wrapping, my hands shook and my vision wavered through a film of sudden tears. Inside the box lay, neatly folded, the coveted chintz quilt from Mama's bed. I buried my face in the folds to take in the lingering scent of my mother, and to add my tears. On top of the quilt was a card:

To my baby sister—my first pick.

René J. Manley

TWO ROCKERS

My sister has two rockers.
She lives in Tennessee
And when I go to visit her
We rock and sip on tea.

The color of her rockers?
A dusty shade of blue.
They're on the porch, beside the door
Where all the folks walk through.

At times we both drink Passionfruit.
At times we sip Earl Grey,

As on the porch we rock and watch
The seasons pass away.

We've talked about our children
We've laughed and cried together
We've sat with sun upon our laps
We've rocked in rainy weather.

Dear Lord, please save two rockers
On the porch called "Glorious Day."
Make hers Eternal Passionfruit.
Make mine the King's Earl Grey.

Charlotte A. Lanham

SISTER BONDING

We began brainstorming two years ago, but somehow it took that long to plan our overnight in New York City. We were dreaming of a mini-vacation exclusively for us without the two husbands we adore and the five children we have mothered. Of course, we see one another often during holiday celebrations and other events but as we've lived in different states for almost twenty-four years, it's hard to experience time together without the din of other people's voices.

My sister is three years older than I am. When we were young, such a gap loomed like an enormous age difference. Was it because I was the middle child who learned to play both sides of the fence? If the world according to my little brother looked like more fun, I'd ally myself with him. If my sister started to enjoy the special privileges that came with her seniority, I'd beg to be included on her agenda.

At times, I drove her crazy. Since our shared closet connected our bedrooms, I could hide on my side and open her door ever so gently to find out how she was dressing for the day. Then I would scramble to imitate her style. For such an intelligent girl, it took her a while to figure out how I could successfully copy her.

Whether they do so consciously or not, parents usually label their children. This was especially true of our parents' generation. My sister was the smart one, while I was the pretty one who still labors to this day to appear like I have a strong mind. My sister continues to fuss with her hair and makeup, and deliberates endlessly about her wardrobe.

We hatched the New York idea because we could catch dinner with our brother who lives there, but also because this city is a logical meeting spot between my home in Boston and hers in Baltimore. Daunted by our busy schedules and raging blizzards that derailed trains and grounded planes, we changed our lodging reservation four times over the course of a year.

Finally on a Tuesday, we were ready to synchronize our watches for our rendezvous. My train arrived at Penn Station miraculously on time; I scrambled outside to hail a cab. As my taxi approached the Soho Grand Hotel, I could see the slick concrete exterior and the bellmen tailored in black from head to toe. For our one night, we were aiming for chic sophistication.

In the lobby, my sister was the first person I saw. Arms open wide, she greeted me with a warm hug. "Did you find it okay? Are you hungry? I'll show you the bathroom." She said all three seemingly in one breath. I was smiling. Perhaps she would always mother me in the kindest of ways.

For our day and a half, we walked the streets of Soho and

Tribeca. We ambled slowly as we luxuriated in our lack of routine or timetable. Behind our dark glasses, which shielded us from the bright sunlight and enabled us to feel like celebrities traveling incognito, we perused storefronts for the perfect shoe as we marveled over chartreuse suede stilettos and leopard slides. We waded through a used clothing emporium searching for vintage purses, and modeled Parisian silk blouses in a fancy boutique where we needed to ring a bell in order to be admitted.

During two-hour lunches, we indulged in praline dessert pastries and cappuccino refills. With no appointments to race to, we focused on one another as we pondered hormone replacement therapy, our aging parents, her upcoming teaching position and my writing career. Thirty years ago while I struggled to keep a horridly unattractive pink picture book hat perched safely on top of my head, my mother pointed out to me: "Even if your friends come and go, your sister will be your friend forever."

Those wise words not only fortified me for my walk down the aisle in front of my sister, the bride, but have also served as a reminder that our relationship is lasting and the confidences we share are secure.

Under fluffy white comforters in our hotel beds, we chatted long into the night and even saw the sky brighten with daylight before we closed our eyes. In the morning, I felt exhausted after a cup of espresso but sweetly fortified for the next six months. Certainly we would figure out another respite with one another. Just the other day I received an e-mail from my sister. While accompanying her husband to New York for a business meeting, she had wandered around Soho by herself only to discover a new hotel for us, one which could possibly be more perfect than the last.

Betsy Banks Epstein

A HOLE IN MY HEART

I was just three and half years old when my dad was killed in a helicopter accident. Even though I do not remember him, I have always felt that his death left a hole in my heart. I have never known how to describe how I feel other than to say that a space was left in my heart that no one else could fill.

A few years ago my mother remarried after being a single mom for a long time. My brother and I were really shocked when she said she wanted another child.

She and my stepfather went through a lot of hard times with infertility to have a baby. Finally after many months, my mom found out she was expecting.

I was not sure at first how it would be with another child in the house because it had always been just my brother and me. My mom chose not to find out if she was having a boy or a girl.

After what seemed like a long time, my mom had a little girl named Bella on Valentine's Day. I had secretly been praying all along for my mom's baby to be a girl. The minute I looked at my little sister I knew she was something special. I think she was a gift to us to bring our two families together.

I realized after a very short time that Bella filled that big hole in my heart that had been there for so long.

Krista Allison, age thirteen

DOUBLY BLESSED

I was sitting in a play yard at a McDonald's restaurant. What little food my five-year-old daughter was going to eat had been eaten and all that was left was the playing.

A handful of children scampered before me. My daughter was somewhere in the mix. After a few moments, she rocketed out of a pit of balls, scattering them everywhere.

"Natalie, be careful," I muttered. She squealed in delight, not hearing a word. She ran toward me panting, "Did you see them?" she asked eagerly.

"Did I see who?" I cringed, nervous I was about to have one of those "my kid said *what*?" type situations.

"Them!" She pointed at two little girls about her age.

"They're the same kid twice!" She announced.

"They aren't the same child twice," I explained, smiling.

"They wear the same clothes," she loudly noted again. "And the same face!" She bellowed completely elated at her discoveries.

"I think they're neat!" she hollered over her shoulder as she ran off.

"Me, too," I said, more to myself than anyone.

"Thank you," came a voice next to me. I turned and realized she was the mother of the twins. She smiled. She seemed unoffended by my daughter's gawking.

In silence we watched them play, my one and her two. I couldn't blame Natalie for being fascinated. They were interesting to watch—and extremely cute in their matching pink outfits and identical haircuts. Even their eyes were the exact same color.

With amusement I noticed that within just mere minutes of retying one of their shoes the other limped over with her laces hanging. And almost in unison their matching barrettes seemed to plop from their heads.

I shrugged. If God could manage the miracle of bringing two identical beings into this world within minutes of each other then simultaneously falling barrettes and untied laces were nothing.

"They really are beautiful," I commented.

She smiled proudly. "Thank you."

We watched in silence a few minutes more while concentrating on the children. The play yard had now emptied except for us.

"They want me to separate them," she announced. I faced her. We weren't parallel talking anymore. We were talking to each other.

"Who?" I asked.

"The school," she frowned. "They go to kindergarten next week and they think it's best for them to be in separate classes."

"What do you think?" I asked.

"I want them to be together," she sighed. As I turned to face her I saw tears welling up in her eyes. I felt bad for her.

"They want you to but they can't make you, right?" I asked, not meaning to oversimplify but instead trying to clarify her situation.

"No, they won't make me. They just 'strongly suggest,'" she said, emphasizing the words. She sighed, testifying that she had been struggling with this for awhile.

"Well, a lot of people 'strongly suggest' a lot of things."

After a small silence she said, "I'm just afraid I'm leading with my heart."

"Well, what else are you supposed to lead with?" For a second it was as if we were old friends. Mother bonding is a special thing.

"You know," she laughed, "psychology and . . . and . . . and . . ."

she couldn't think of anything else. We laughed together.

Relaxing, we watched our children play. I couldn't help but notice their mannerisms were the same. They hopped on the same foot, chose the same hiding place, held the same pose for freeze tag and giggled the very same giggle.

All of a sudden I cared deeply about them staying together. It would be wrong to separate them.

I faced the mother. "Think of it this way," I said. "We spend our entire lives trying to find someone like us. We spend our entire lives looking for a best friend. Someone who likes and dislikes the same things we do, someone to be there for us, someone who's known us from the start," speaking hurriedly, grasping now for anything that might move her. "Heck, someone to sit with at lunch."

"It looks to me," I said, "that they were born with what the rest of us spend our whole lives looking for. If you happen to be that blessed, why should you change it?"

She faced me. Her eyes were wide. I had touched her.

"Are you a twin?" she asked.

"No," I said shaking my head.

"You have a sister?" she pressed, sure that I did.

"No," I said. As I spoke the word, I realized that I had learned something about myself I never knew before. Something I had kept hidden inside my own heart.

"I'm just someone who always wished she had," I explained. A lump formed in my throat and my eyes filled with tears.

There wasn't much left to say. My mind flickered back to memories of my childhood when I would play in my closet with my make-believe sister. Memories I had long forgotten.

We watched the kids a couple more minutes. Then almost together we checked our watches and said, "We better get going."

"Thank you," she said softly. I could tell it was from the heart.

"Girls," she called them. They ran to her. One at a time they scampered to her side. She turned them toward me.

"Tell the lady 'thank you.'"

Dutifully, having no idea what they were thanking me for, they mimicked her thank you with such an exact pitch that it sounded as if it were one voice.

I laughed. They were amazingly cute.

"You're welcome," I answered. Leaning down to their level I whispered loud enough for their mother to hear, "Stick together."

"They will," she said, smiling at me.

Walking to the car Natalie asked, "Will I ever have a twin?"

"No," I said, buckling her into the seatbelt. "You have to be born together, remember?"

"Right," she said.

"Will I ever have a sister?" she asked as we drove out of the parking lot.

"No," I said again, watching her in the rearview mirror. "I'm sorry you won't."

"I'm like you," she reasoned. "You never had a sister either, huh, Mommy?"

"No honey, I didn't," I said, feeling a little bad for both of us.

"Well," she said, with the optimistic wisdom of a five-year-old, "if I ever would have had a sister I would have really loved her."

As I watched her drift off to sleep, I thought, *I would have, too.*

Christine Pisera Naman

MY SISTER'S EYEBROWS

It was more than forty years ago that my big sister Marcella and I had the conversation about eyebrows. I was a little girl and she was a blossoming young woman. She was sitting at her vanity preparing to go out when she looked over at me, laughed and said, "You're the girl with no eyebrows!"

"I am not!" I retorted. But I knew she was right. My eyebrows were just stuck there above my eyes, sparse and straight, with no arch.

I often sat next to her vanity like that with my chin cupped in my hands, watching her "going out" ritual. First came eye shadow, then eyeliner on those marvelous mossy-green eyes. Pretty containers with swirled names like Maybelline and Cover

Girl opened and closed with clicks and twists. Sometimes she would reach over and dab Chanel No. 5, Seven Winds or White Shoulders perfume on my neck. This anointing was like a promise that one day I would be a young woman, too.

The finishing touch to her face was always the same. She picked up a tiny brush and shaped her perfectly arched eyebrows. They were the most beautiful eyebrows I had ever seen.

Sliding into the seat in front of her vanity mirror after she had gone, I looked at my plain face. There were those cursed straight eyebrows. I was missing eyelashes that were stuck on the eyelash curler. I wore an ugly hand-me-down knit shirt that belonged to my brother and my pigtails were a mess. I would never be pretty like her even though her perfume promised something more.

On Saturdays she occasionally passed the time with me sitting on the sofa going through the pages of ladies dresses in the Sears catalog. Her long graceful finger with pearl nail-polish pointed out the dresses she liked. When I picked my favorite, it had polka dots or ruffles—or better yet, both. Her raised eyebrow and a non-committal "hmmm" started me looking beyond the flash and frills of things in life.

In a family of short, round people it was odd she was statuesque—nearly six feet tall. She purchased clothes at exclusive stores. I remember a sharkskin skirt, a rust-colored camel hair coat, a sable stole she saved up for and glass-heeled shoes covered with black lace.

Marcella introduced me to classical music and showed me how to twirl spaghetti on a spoon like a lady. When I turned thirteen, she took Mother's sewing scissors and cut my long braided hair. I looked so different, and perfume didn't seem too far-fetched anymore.

I grew up, married and moved away from my family. As the years passed, Marcella's stunning dark hair turned into stunning silver and she never lost her sense of style. There was always a special feeling between the two of us that our distance from each other never changed.

Marcella got cancer in her early fifties. Her treatment was so successful that the family went back into normal life soon after. Twelve years later the news came that her cancer had returned. She went shopping for new clothes saying, "I'm going to go in style when I go to the doctor's appointments."

The chemo took her hair and eyebrows and she became emaciated. I thought about the vanity mirror, the makeup, the perfume and my beautiful green-eyed sister. The next day I bought pale pink tissue paper. In it I wrapped pink nailpolish the shade of seashells, lacy pink underwear, glossy pink lipstick and cosmetics in pretty containers. The last thing I wrapped was eyebrow powder and a tiny brush. Like the dab of perfume she put on my neck all those years ago, the little pink packages were my promise to carry for her the hope of things she couldn't yet see.

We vacationed at the ocean a few weeks later and returned the next year and then the next. We sat on the porch steps eating mounds of ice cream, collected seashells everyday and watched shooting stars at night. That's how I want to remember her.

Marcella fought cancer for two more years. Three weeks before she died, she ordered new clothes from a catalog. I know I'll smile about that some day. We dressed her in the 24-karat gold stockings she loved, a symbolic gesture recognizing her courageous struggle to meet cancer head on and give it her all.

Linda L. S. Knouse

ONLY THE TWO OF US IN SIGHT

Grandma lived only a few blocks from the Daytona Boardwalk, close enough to smell the salt in the air and feel the ocean breezes rustle the palms in our yard as if waving to us. My sister Josie and I spent long summers there. We took off for a day at the beach every chance we could. Josie let the screen door whap shut as we headed down the steps in our sun-faded bathing suits. No shoes. No towels. *Oo, oo, ooh*ing and *ah, ah, ahh*ing all the way past the stucco and oyster-shell houses in the alley. I can close my eyes and see myself at the age of three trotting to keep up with Josie over the blistering pavement as we passed stores that sold cheesy, airbrushed T-shirts displaying Daytona and drippy sunsets. My sister was twelve and I thought she knew everything.

Josie squeezed my sweaty palm and took in a deep breath before stepping down onto the busy intersection. Glancing from side to side, she inched us along the highway, weaving between bumpers and tourists honking their horns. After making it to the shaded sidewalk and concrete barrier wall, we released our pent-up breath; her grip loosened and the feeling slowly came back into my tingling fingers. The powdered sand stuck to our scorched feet offering no relief. We hopped to the first tidal pool and wiggled our toes in the tepid, shallow water.

Josie took me up the stairs and onto the boardwalk where retired couples in straw hats and with zinc-white noses strolled, stopping to take turns posing for a picture by the famous pier. We waved to the carnival workers busy helping the children and parents in and out of cable cars. I pulled back on Josie's hand to make her stop so that I could look up at the cars lifting over our heads, watching the kids' dangling flip-flops moving out to sea.

We stopped to say hello to our worn-out friend, Pappy, a stooped-over leathery man with shaky hands and a stubbled chin. He wore a dingy apron into which the tourist children dropped quarters to ride Pedro, his faithful donkey and money-making partner. I never got to ride Pedro. We did not have quarters to bring to the beach. But we patted Pedro's cushioned nose and Josie lifted me to stroke his stiff, fuzzy ears.

I wandered down to the edge and dug my toes into the slick sand, plopping down in front of the little waves that lapped and foamed around my bottom. Josie would grab my hand, swinging me up on her hip with a "Whee!" I clung to her like a spider monkey, my arms and legs wrapped tight.

"Loosen up, you're choking me." She pried my arms loose.

"I'm scared. Don't go so deep." I buried my face in her neck and squeezed.

"Don't be such a baby. I've got you good and tight. Get ready. . . . Jump!"

We leaped up and let the wave slap our stomachs and chests. Josie wrapped her arms around my waist and twirled in the ocean making giant circles. I laughed and giggled, all dizzy, as the waters swirled and pressed around us in a kaleidoscope of land and sea. We played and played, each wave swelling higher and higher, making it harder for Josie to keep her balance. We tumbled in the whoosh of the surf. The angry waves bulged and buckled, knocking us back with its mighty force. The undertow dragged us out to sea, prying me from my sister's arms. Her grip slipped.

Josie scrambled for me, arms flailing, nails clawing to keep a hold. I sunk, ears filling with water, muffling our fighting sounds. I opened my mouth to scream, water rushed in and down my throat, seemingly anxious to fill hollow spaces. I searched, head turning from side to side in the blurry water. Where was my Josie?

Looking up, the shimmering distorted light called to me in the unreachable distance. I thrashed and fought but sunk further down, hit bottom with a thud, hip and thigh scraping grit and shell. I pushed at the water, as if it were a sheet on grandma's laundry line, hoping her smiling face would appear. Something solid brushed against my wrist. I felt fingers grasping then slipping in the salt water. Then she was gone. My throat burned, and the waters swirled black as I sunk further from the light.

Fingers tugged at my hair, touched my face, my jaw and moved to my bathing suit strap, hooked it and yanked me up, grabbing my tangled hair along, lifting me through the surging waters. My head broke free into the air and light. I sputtered and coughed, gagged and sneezed. Josie pounded my back, her shrieks filled my ears. A blur of people rushed toward us, concerned faces, offering arms. Josie shook her head no, and held me tighter. She rushed to shore, my body jolted against hers in the run. As the sea splashed and swished about her legs, her feet plodded onto wet sand. She dropped to her knees. I clutched tighter, refusing to let go.

I cried and gulped air until burps and belches bubbled in release. Josie rocked and shushed me. Josie tucked me in her arms and legs, closer and closer. I held on, hooking my legs around her stomach, my arms around her chest, goose-bumped and shivering in the warm, late afternoon sun. I heard Josie whisper, "Don't tell Grandma, all right? She would worry about us and not let me bring you to the beach again—you wanna be able to come to the beach with me, don't you?"

Her words trembled. I nodded hard and sucked the salt out of a lock of hair plastered against my cheek. Josie went back to rocking me, resting her chin on top of my head. I laid my head against her chest, listening to her heart—*tha . . . thump . . . tha . . . thump*—answer mine.

At sunset, Josie and I walked the shore under a rose-washed sky. Happy and silent—only the two of us in sight. We played the game of smashing the foam and stamping out the clam air bubbles with our big toes, counting to see who got the most. Our feet hit concrete only when the last rays of light dimmed and the ache for food called us home.

We ate—eyeing each other across the table in silent understanding. Josie bathed me and we stood at our grandma's bedroom door and told her good night, focusing on the red glow of her one, nightly cigarette. At dark we slid between the white sheets and lay with our faces close to the screens, cooled by the mist from evening thunderstorms. As sleep moved over me, I felt the pulse of the waves nudging, swaying and rocking me to sleep in rhythm with the sounds of the nearby sea.

Carol D. O'Dell

IN SEARCH OF A SIMPLER TIME

We were partners in crime. What started as mischief became a yearly ritual we looked forward to every Christmas.

There were more children than money in our large family, but every year our parents managed to make Christmas a celebration to be remembered.

But one of my fondest Christmas memories is the secret shared only with my older sister, Barbara.

Our crime was committed while shopping for our siblings. Our father would give us a crisp $5 bill with stern instructions that it was to be spent only on presents for our sisters, then drop us at the nearest dime store, with instructions to shop and then wait by the door until he returned. Once our shopping was completed, Barbara and I would sneak to the soda counter, climb up on the tall round stools, plunk down our leftover change and count to see if we had enough. We always did. Grinning, we ordered hot fudge sundaes, then sat there, conspirators in crime, skinny legs dangling as we giggled and licked the thick, gooey chocolate from our spoons.

Fast-forward fifty years. Barbara was diagnosed with incurable cancer. We were told there was no cure, but "palliative therapy" would make her more comfortable. Every day for weeks, particles of energy were bombarded through her brain. Fatigue and nausea became daily companions. Next, chemotherapy, with all its unpleasant side effects. However, with the help of new medications, soon we were pleasantly surprised to find that Barbara no longer experienced nausea. Her appetite even returned. That is when we began our quest. We were determined to find the perfect match of our childhood memory. The ice cream must be the hard kind, the harder the better, since the thick, hot fudge will cause it to melt right away. It had to have a cherry on top and it absolutely must be in a glass dish shaped like a tulip. That was the recipe.

We spent the entire time she was in treatment in search of the absolutely perfect concoction. We didn't tell anyone else what we were doing; once again it was our secret.

Treatment day was always Monday; by evening she could barely keep her eyes open. The week became a blur of growing fatigue, confusion and weakness, but by the weekend, Barbara would begin to rally and by Sunday she was ready.

"You think we will find it this time?" she'd ask. We'd laugh then climb into the car.

We ate a lot of ice cream that year, but it always seemed something was slightly off-kilter. Soft ice cream wasn't the same as the hard-packed we remembered, chocolate syrup didn't give the same sensual delight as the thick goo of our childhood, the cherry on top was missing, or even worse, it was served in a paper container. The exact replica seemed impossible to find. Week after week we searched for the perfect combination. We were on a mission—in search of a childhood memory and a simpler time.

"We didn't find it, did we?" Barbara sighed one morning. I knew exactly what she meant.

"No, but we're not giving up!" I replied. "Are you up for a road trip?"

The next day we took a longer trip than any we had previously attempted.

By the time we arrived at the ice cream parlor bedecked in 1950s décor, she was drained. She needed help just to get out of the car.

As the waitress held out menus, Barbara spoke softly. "We won't need those. We already know what we want—hot fudge sundaes. Do you use hard ice cream?"

"Of course," the waitress replied.

Barbara beamed at me. "I think that we might have found it."

Soon the waitress returned carrying two tall tulip-shaped glasses filled with cold, hard, vanilla ice cream smothered in rich, thick hot fudge sauce, topped with a squirt of whipped cream and a cherry. "Is this what you wanted?" she asked as she plunked them down on the counter.

I turned toward my sister. Our eyes locked. The silent, secret question hung in the air between us. *Was it?* Slowly we picked up our spoons, plunged them into the sweet, cold confection and took them to our mouths. As I licked the thick, rich chocolate goo from my lips, I looked toward Barbara and saw she was doing the same. We began to first smile, and then giggle.

Mission accomplished. There we were—not two overweight, middle-aged women enjoying an afternoon dessert with more calories than either needed. We were two giggling little girls, perched on high stools, skinny legs dangling, sharing the precious bond of sisterhood, carried back to a time when life was simple and "palliative treatment," were just words that had no meaning.

Nancy Harless

THE WAGON

Last month on her sixty-third birthday, I reminded my sister of the following incident. She asked if I remembered it or if it were just part of our family lore. I'm not sure, but I do remember a ride in our red wagon.

Adored by her parents, aunts and uncles, for the first sixteen months of her life my elder sister basked in the attention that is showered on an only child. Then I arrived on the scene, and she had to divide that attention with a red-faced, bawling little creature who needed quiet times for sleep and craved to be held in her mother's arms.

As we grew older, we often fought over rights to panda bears and other toys meant for our mutual enjoyment. Exasperated by our constant bickering, my parents finally told my sister, "If you can't play nice and share the toys with your little sister, we're going to give Beverly away to your cousin Jerry."

My sister knew a good thing when she heard it. One day as I continued to encroach on her territory, she put me in our little red wagon and began to pull it along the sidewalk. Coming to a corner she was not supposed to cross by herself, she waited. Our mother came running down to the street corner, yelling, "Stop!" After she caught her breath, she asked my sister, "Marilyn, where are you going?"

"I'm taking Bee to Jerry's house; he can have her!"

Beverly McLaggan

MY SISTER, MYSELF

The first time I visit my father's bungalow at the University of Nigeria, I perch on a vinyl settee in the parlor and drink milky tea while my father rambles on about the student riots, the military government's Structural Adjustment Program, his college years with my mother, what he recalls her saying about her family's farm in Washington State—never a pause for me or anyone else to speak.

Meanwhile my stepmother, another stranger, flits about the room, dipping forward with black-market sugar and tins of Danish biscuits, slipping coasters under our cups the instant we lift to sip. From the darkened hallway come the slap of flip-flops and giggles.

"You have children?" I ask politely, as if this were a question for a daughter to ask her father, as if it were not the question I traveled halfway around the globe to ask.

When I was not quite two, my father, a graduate student from Nigeria, returned home, leaving clothes and books scattered across the floor of his rented room. He was to attend to family business, scout out job prospects and come back. Though my parents had split, and my mother was raising me alone in Seattle, she maintained relations with my father for my sake. "I want you to know that this is not a good-bye," he wrote to us from a ship in the middle of the Atlantic, nervous about reports of ethnic and religious tensions awaiting him. "I shall look forward to our meeting so long as we are all alive." My mother never saw him again.

Now, more than two decades later, my stepmother nods at my question and glances at my father. She is light-skinned and solicitous, with a wide nose and a voice like the breeze of the fans she angles at me.

"Yes, yes, there are children." My father waves his hands. "You'll meet them later." He is short like me, his weathered skin dark as plums. A strip of wiry black hair encircles the back of his head. There's a space in his mouth where a tooth should be. I don't see the broad-shouldered rugby player who stared out from my wall all those years. The only feature I recognize is that round nose.

A blur flashes tan and red in the hallway. I glance up to see a velvety-brown girl in a scarlet school uniform receding into the dimness, familiar eyes stunned wide in a face I could swear is mine.

It's not possible, I tell myself. Even if the girl in the hall is my sister, we have different mothers of different races. How can we look so alike? For twenty-six years I have been an only child, the only black member of our family, our town.

My father explains that during Christmas we'll travel to our ancestral village, where I will be formally presented to the extended family and clan elders. I do not mention that for me Christmas has always been white.

After my mother moved from Seattle to my grandparents' farm, I grew up hearing Finnish spoken, with a wreath of candles in my curls on St. Lucia Day. Mummi, my Finnish grandmother, and I spent all December at the kitchen table cutting out *nissu,* cookies in the shape of pigs and six-point stars from the almond-scented dough. Before baking, we painted them with tiny brushes, like the ones Mummi used for tinting family photographs. Sheet after sheet of cookies emerged from the oven transformed, the egg paint set in a deep satiny glaze.

Each night Old Pappa, my Swedish grandfather, and I built snow lanterns in the yard for the *tonttu,* farm sprites, and I imagined that we were conductors on the Underground Railroad, lighting the way for runaway slaves.

I spent my childhood at the window waiting for Anansi the Spider and Loki the Half-Giant, tricksters from my African folktales and Norse legends, to come scuttling over the purple mountains that ringed the farm. They would say, "Welcome, sister!" in a special language that only we understood. But no one ever came. No one has ever looked like me. Until now.

In true African fashion, my new parents and I move slowly, circuitously, as if conversation were a tribal praise song with instrumental flourishes and digressive harmonies. Eventually my father calls, "Emeka, Okechukwu, Adanna! Come and greet your sister!"

Even before the words leave his mouth, the three are quivering in the center of the parlor. Grins split their faces. The eldest boy, Emeka, is already languid with teenage charisma. Behind him stoops a lanky boy with yellow skin and glittering, feverish eyes: Okechukwu. Pressed close to his side is twelve-year-old Adanna. She is me, fourteen years ago.

"Okay," our father says, the Igbo chieftain making clan policy, "this is your older sister from America. She's come to visit. You love her." With one sentence, I go from being the sole daughter, niece, grandchild to being the eldest of four, the one with the responsibility for love.

Adanna reaches me first. She is exquisite—luminous skin the color of Dutch cocoa; heart-shaped face with high, rounded cheekbones, slimmer than mine; a mouth that flowers above a delicate pointed chin. We come face-to-face, and the rest of the family gasps, steps back, and makes way for us. I can see myself for the first time—we are exquisite.

"I've missed you," I tell her. She gleams.

Later, during the brief calm before the arrival of relatives, she will lie with her head in my lap and stare at me: Elder sister. One who spoils. Exotic American. Passport to what lies ahead, whom she will become. And I will stare back at her: Younger sister. One who adores. Exotic African. Passport back home, to what I have always been.

Faith Adiele

BENEATH THE STARS

Under our tent of blankets and clothes—pinned to the line,
my sister and I believed we were miles away from home
though we were only in the backyard.

Holding hands we watched the tree shadows
create wild images and marveled that we were
sleeping outside instead of in our crowded bed.

The dogs peeked their heads inside our tent
while the neighbors played their accordions and guitars,
serenading us to sleep beneath the silent stars.

Diane Payne

ET, TU, MY PERFECT SISTER

I've got one of *those* sisters—you know the type—she's "perfect." A perfect size 8 who always had her bed perfectly made, her hair perfectly coifed, and always got perfect test scores in grade school. As a child, I could spot that look in my teachers' eyes when they came across my name on the attendance sheet and realized I was the younger sister of their former, beloved, "perfect" student, Michele. I also knew how quickly that gleam of contentment would fade to one of squinting disappointment once my educational achievements (or lack thereof) would come to light.

"You know Jodi, your sister, Michele, always got 100 percent on her spelling tests," the teacher would start, "and her penmanship—why it was simply. . ." here it comes, ". . . perfect!" I'd mouth in unison. Ugh! Michele, Michele, Michele! I love my sister, but having to follow her in school—man, I could definitely relate to Jan Brady!

But eventually we grew up and I stepped out of my perfect sister's shadow. And now I feel it's time to set the record straight. Picture it—Pennsylvania, 1985. I was still in college and living at home at the time, and Michele, now married (to, yes, the "perfect" man), had returned home for a visit. As all of our reunions ultimately turn out, hours of reminiscing over old stories, one spilling into the next, left us literally rolling on the floor in hysterics and crying tears of laughter. On this particular day, our high jinks led us into the only forbidden room in our mother's home—the living room. From the sofa that was never sat on for more than a few seconds to take family photos, to its countless statues and figurines, this room resembled a museum more than a living room, and it was an unwritten rule that it was "off limits, except for company." I'm not sure what started this particular chain of events, but the next thing I knew, Michele was juggling couch pillows, one came careening at my head, I ducked, and then there was a thud followed by a crash. Our laughter and horseplay immediately ground to a halt as we turned around silently. There, lying on the floor, was our mother's cherished, black, ceramic bust of Julius Caesar—decapitated!

"Ohhh! You're in trouble now!" I couldn't help squealing.

"Oh for Pete's sake, I'm an adult, what's she going to do, ground me?" Michele retorted.

"Well, there was that time she grounded you for a month—two weeks before you got married," I reminded her which instantly set us both of into hysterics again.

"Okay, okay! Quick, help me glue his head on," the perfect sister begged between sobs of laughter.

Working together, we used an entire bottle of Elmer's glue and finally repositioned Caesar's head back in place. And after we inked in the cracks with a black magic marker, it didn't look half bad in our desperate minds.

"There, Mom will never know," Michele said as she carefully placed the statue back onto the marble stand where he had sat untouched (except for his weekly dusting) for the past seven years since mom had gotten the hideous figure—I mean, work of art—for Christmas.

The next few hours were spent patting ourselves on the back and winking and smirking about the day's events all through dinner. Yes, we were home free—but that was until Caesar's head fell off two hours later during a family photo session and rolled across the floor, landing at our mother's feet.

I'm sure no real punishment was doled out over "the incident" as we now refer to it in our family, but just to set the record straight, it was the perfect sister who delivered the "deadly" blow to poor Caesar—I was merely a party to the crime.

Jodi Severson

THE BOLOGNA WARS

My younger sister and I were dyed-in-the-wool tomboys. When our family moved from the small fenced yards of big city living to the freedom of the country, we thought we had landed on our own little patch of heaven. We spent hours playing in the barn, walking the fields and riding our bikes down the gravel road that eventually reached a tiny town if you went the whole five miles. Near our house the road crossed a little stream that pooled on one side where a school of fish had made their home. The largest was probably only about six inches long, but to our childish eyes they all looked like twelve-pound salmon.

On occasion we would venture into the small town library and check out books. We would lie in the grass and read and then integrate the stories into our own adventures. Once we checked out a book about "The Pioneers." That one really snagged our imaginations. The rolling Missouri farmland surrounding us was the ideal setting to hack out a life for ourselves with our bare hands. So with the exception of television and bathrooms, which we were sure the pioneers would have gladly used had they had them, we determined to renounce the trappings of modern society and live off the land.

We rounded up all the fallen branches we could find and fashioned ourselves a log cabin. It was the perfect house in which to live a pioneering life, at one with nature, despite the trivial inconvenience that it had no roof. Next we addressed the food situation. Our mother kept a garden, so vegetables were no problem, but what about meat? My sister and I stared at each other, as the same thought dawned on us—*the fish!* It didn't matter that we gagged and whined every time our mother made us eat it. Our fish would taste great because they would be fresh! Fishing could become our contribution to the family welfare. We'd bring some home every night and save our parents gobs of money on groceries.

We scrounged around until we found an old badminton net pole and tied some string onto it. Then we filched one of our baby sister's diaper pins to use as a hook. Now, bait. It seemed mean and really icky to skewer a worm on that sharp pin. Instead, we bummed half a slice of bologna from the fridge. Since it was a hot afternoon, we knew the fish would be dying for a nice cool piece of meat. With our fishing pole, bait and confidence in hand, we proudly made a beeline to the pond.

Since I was the eldest, I solemnly informed my sister that I would hold the pole. Fishing was tricky business and since our family's fortunes apparently hinged upon our ability to master it, it should be handled by someone who knew what she was doing. Wide eyed, she acquiesced. So we baited the hook, dropped it into the water and hunched on the shoulder of the road, me holding the pole and my sister sitting quietly.

As we stared at the spot where our string disappeared into the pool, we saw a little shudder. In the heat of the moment, my sister grabbed the metal rod with both hands as the string gave a tremendous tug. We had a bite! Excitedly, we jerked the pole up with our combined strength and whipped the string hard enough that the diaper pin sailed over our heads and landed on the road behind us. We spun around to admire our whopper to find not only no fish, but no bologna as well. Perplexed, we looked at the hook, at the water, and at the hook again. Then we gathered up our stuff and dejectedly walked home.

By the time we got there, we figured out that we must have pulled the line up way too hard. I pointed out that that's why it was best to have just one designated pole holder. My sister saw the wisdom in this and promised to work on her self-control. We had fried chicken for dinner that night. We told our parents to enjoy that chicken because by the next day, it'd be fresh fish every night.

The next afternoon, with our bologna, we marched back to the pool. We sat on the hot road, dangling our feet over the water and waited for dinner to bite. Then my sister saw something move on the bank and we pulled our feet up, mindful of the snakes that roamed the countryside. It wasn't a snake though; it was a frog. And he must have been one of those nuclear-radiation-mutant kinds because he was about as big and round as a saucer. While we watched, he slipped into the water, swam over to our line and dove out of sight. Suddenly, the string started dancing and I yanked it out of the water. The pin swung in little circles, naked as a jaybird. We looked at each other indignantly. That big, stupid frog had stolen our bait! We'd see about that.

We stuck more bologna on the hook, dropped the line back in the pond, and then bombarded the water with gravel, hoping to stone the thieving thing as it tried again. After a minute we stopped throwing rocks and, panting and sweaty, scanned the banks to see if the slimy critter had washed up anywhere. While we were thus engaged, the pole jerked in my hand. I lifted the pin out of the water. Empty! We walked home bickering about whose fault all this was and that night could barely bring ourselves to touch our meatloaf and mashed potatoes.

Like all serious pioneers, we didn't let our setbacks dampen our spirits. The next day we were ready to get at it again. We were determined to catch a fish because our mother had told us that this would be our last piece of bologna—we were apparently feeding all our dad's luncheon meat to the frog. We prudently quartered the bologna, and after checking out the shoreline and lobbing a few rocks for good measure, we dropped the pin into the water and waited.

Ten minutes into it, we regretfully decided that the fish must not be hungry and that we should save our dwindling supply of bait for another day. I drew up the line and, to our amazement, the hook was clean as a whistle. This meant war! We knew we were going to have to catch the frog or we'd get nary a minnow out of that pond. So we dangled our second piece of meat just under the surface where we could snatch it up the second that greedy frog got his mouth around our bait. We stared at that pin so intently, we saw the exact moment the frog floated up like some ugly Macy's Thanksgiving Day parade balloon and ripped the meat right off the hook. As he sank back down, he seemed to waggle the bologna at us.

A few weeks after this, we were driving into town with our mom. As we passed our old stomping grounds, we looked over nostalgically and, lo and behold, sitting nice as you please on the side of the road was Mr. Big Stupid Frog himself. On our turf! We screamed at our mom to stop the car, which she did, skidding on the gravel. We eased out of the car, thinking that if we could take the old croaker prisoner, we'd finally be the queens of the pond. We circled the frog gingerly, step-by-step, effectively cutting him off from a watery escape. Still he sat there. Inching up, we nervously squatted over him. The two of us posed in frozen uncertainty for a minute, then my adoring little sister looked up at me expectantly. I looked at the creepy monster. Terror must have rooted him to the spot because he hadn't moved a muscle. Holding my breath, I was stretching one finger forward to give the frog a good poke when the totally unexpected happened. He attacked, lunging straight for my face and leaving us with no other option than to scream and run away.

We dove into the backseat, slammed the door shut and sat glumly, contemplating our failure during the ride into town. Once there, we went straight to the library and checked out a book on how to become space cadets. Living off the land was for the birds anyway, and dangerous to boot. No wonder all the pioneers were dead.

Tanith Nicole Tyler

DEAREST MARGARET

Yes, we've agreed, when we grow newly old
to live side by side on your farm in Vermont
where we can raise goats
the small brown kind, following close
and bleating of love.
We've said we want cats, all colors of cats
to play in the shade on hot summer days,
to purr by the stove when evenings are cold.
And, Margaret, remember our plan to grow plants
with long Latin names
and prizewinning Bibb lettuce
for good-tasting salads.
You'll make tabbouleh (you do it so well).
I'll roast a capon (with shallots and beans).
How well we will dine

drinking mint tea or watered white wine
followed by cheese and sweet almonds.
Indeed, we can travel
wherever we like
as long as we're home by noon
to pet the cats, feed the goats
water the prizewinning lettuce.
When winter snow falls
we will pull on tall boots and warm, wooly coats
and slosh down our paths to the tin mailbox
by the side of the road.
To the postman we'll offer our best apple tart
hot from the oven with cream
in exchange for choice letters.
(We'll write them ourselves!)
Oh, Margaret, let's read Ulysses
(again) and this time, patient with age,
unravel the prose of James Joyce.

Eleanor Byers

CONTRIBUTORS

Faith Adiele teaches nonfiction at the University of Pittsburgh and travel writing at the Iowa Summer Writing Festival. Her books include a memoir, *Meeting Faith: The Forest Journals of a Black Buddhist Nun in Thailand* (Norton, 2004), and a mystery thriller, *The Student Body (www.thestudentbody.com)*. Contact her at: *www.pitt.edu/~adiele*.

Krista Allison is the daughter of the late Davey Allison, who competed in the NASCAR Winston Cup series. Davey lost his life tragically in 1993, when Krista was just three years old. Krista lives in Nashville, Tennessee, with her family. She is a cheerleader at her school and loves to sew.

Renée Brouillette is an attorney who lives in Roseville, California. She writes to celebrate family and history. Her nonfiction has appeared in *Dog Fancy, Doll Reader* and *The Antique Trader*. She is working on her first novel.

Vivian Eisenecher holds a degree in business administration (magna cum laude), and a certificate in gerontology. Her published works include stories in *Chicken Soup for the Single's Soul, Woman's World, Viewpoint* and *Writer's News*. She has also completed a 250-page suspense novel in which such topics as addiction, incest and recovery are an integral part. She is currently employed in the marketing department at Palomar Pomerado Health and is a copywriter in her spare time. Mother to one daughter, Kim, and one son, Todd, she makes her home in San Diego, California, with her husband and two cats. She loves to read, write, travel and take long walks.

Betsy Banks Epstein writes social commentary and travel articles. Her work has appeared in the *Boston Sunday Globe,* the *Burlington Free Press, Booming* magazine, *Pandemonium,* an anthology of parental humor, and *The Walker Within,* a collection of inspirational stories. She is a regular *Cambridge Chronicle* columnist and lives in Cambridge.

Nancy Harless is a nurse practitioner now exercising her menopausal zest through travel, volunteering in various health-care projects and writing about those experiences. Most of her writing is done in a towering maple tree, in the treehouse built specifically for that purpose by her husband, Norm. She is currently writing a book about some of the strong and beautiful women she has met along her journey. E-mail: *nancyharless@hotmail.com*.

Linda L. S. Knouse was born and raised in the Allegheny Mountains of western Pennsylvania. She currently resides in eastern Pennsylvania near Philadelphia. She is the youngest of nine children. Her sister, Marcella, is the topic of her story in this book. Linda writes about her family, family issues and nature. She can be reached at *linda@knouses.net*.

Charlotte Lanham lives in Duncanville, Texas, with her husband, Ray. She is a freelance writer, former columnist and a contributor to *Chicken Soup for the Mother & Daughter Soul*. She is also the co-founder of Abbi's Room, a non-profit organization that provides bed and bedding for children of Habitat for Humanity families. E-mail: *charlotte.lanham@sbcglobal.net*.

René Manley is a writer and child development specialist in Salem, Oregon. She holds a master's degree in counseling and writes for and about children and families. The author of a weekly newspaper column, *Friend of the Family,* you may reach her at *renemanley@comcast.net*.

Beverly McLaggan recently retired from teaching and counseling in San Jose, California. She enjoys reading, traveling, discussing books and playing piano. Currently, she is working on a novel and in the future plans to write a children's book illustrated by her husband. Please reach her at: *rmclaggan@earthlink.net*.

Christine Pisera Naman is a writer and stay-at-home mom. She lives in Monroeville, Pennsylvania, with her husband and three children. Her first book, *Faces of Hope,* a book featuring babies born on September 11, 2001, was published in 2002.

Carol D. O'Dell has been published in magazines and anthologies including *Atlanta Magazine* and *Jacksonville Magazine*. She lives with her husband and three daughters in Jacksonville,

Florida. "Only the Two of Us in Sight" is an excerpt from her completed memoir, *Said Child*. Contact her at *writecarol@juno.com* for her Web address.

Diane Payne is waiting for Red Hen Press to publish her memoir *Burning Tulips*. Her agent, Erin Reel, is looking for a publisher for her short story collection "Maps and Detours." Every summer, she and her daughter get together with her sister and her two children, and once again, they sleep beneath the stars.

Jodi Severson earned a bachelor's degree in psychology from the University of Pittsburgh. She resides in Rice Lake, Wisconsin, with her husband and three beautiful children. Her stories have been published in *Chicken Soup for the Working Woman's Soul, Chicken Soup for the Sister's Soul, US Legacies Magazine* and Honoring Our Ancestors. Reach her at: *jodis@charter.net*.

Tanith Nicole Tyler is an aspiring writer who lives in Richmond, California, with her husband, Donnell Gordon, their three dogs and Oliver the cockatoo. When not writing, Tanith enjoys delivering Meals on Wheels, remodeling, reading and hiking with her pets. Please reach her at: *tanithtyler@yahoo.com*.